"It is quite simply an honour to be working with Bombay Sapphire. Why? Because Bombay Sapphire is unquestionably the finest gin. And as gin is by far the most interesting mixing spirit, I'm in my element. In concocting, inventing, tasting these drinks I couldn't be happier."

Jamie Walker
The Bombay Sapphire Experience at Vinopolis

To experience the true cocktail experience, it is important that the right ingredients are used. For the best quality cocktails, take care to use BOMBAY SAPPHIRE gin, and MARTINI vermouth products. While the complete names are not always used, please note that the terms BOMBAY SAPPHIRE, BOMBAY and SAPPHIRE are used only to refer to BOMBAY SAPPHIRE gin. MARTINI is used to refer only to genuine MARTINI vermouth products. Where the term 'martini' is used in lower case only, it is meant to simply refer to the martini type of cocktail.

Content

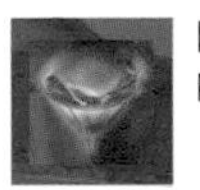

Page 1
Foreword

Page 4
Introduction

Page 10
Cocktail history and culture

Page 18
Vinopolis and Bombay Sapphire

Page 20
The Bombay Sapphire 1763 martini
Bombay Sapphire classic martinis and cocktails

Page 22
Jamie Walker
An introduction to Bombay Sapphire's mixologist

Page 24
Jamie Walker's Sapphire Facets
Bombay Finbar, Sapphire and Emerald, Sapphire Scratch

Page 28
Miami bar feature
Tides - Miami

Page 32
Jamie Walker's Sapphire Sophistication
Black Antoinette, Black Forest Sapphire, Bombay Drago

Page 36
West London bar feature
Art Bar - South Kensington, Townhouse - Knightsbridge

Page 40
Jamie Walker's Sapphire Comforters
The Elegant Ellis, The Keats Sapphire, Wenceslas Sapphire

Page 44
Tokyo bar feature
B-bar - Roppongi Hills, The Peak Bar - Park Hyatt

Page 48
Jamie Walker's Natural Sapphires
Sapphire Shogun, Rosemary's Sapphire Infusion, Barbed Bombay

Page 52
East London bar feature
Vic Naylor - St John Street, Cicada - St John Street

Page 56
Jamie Walker's Sapphire Specialities
Bombay Rouge, Masked Devil of Bombay, Starsky Sapphire

Page 60
Spanish bar feature
Dry Martini Bar - Barcelona
Museo Chicote - Madrid

Page 64
Jamie Walker's Sapphire Luxuries
Bombay Lemon Bomb, Bombay Split, Sapphire Wozzy

Page 68
Mixology
Jamie Walker's tools and techniques

Cocktails make the most of a moment, more than any other drink. They draw a hundred things into a single second, and set it alight.

When it's right, it's wonderful.

Many things are involved. The sense of place: the ambiance, from the lighting to the seats. The company: a familiar smile, a light in the eye. The recipe: the right ingredients brought together, just so. And the preparation itself: sometimes elaborate, often discreet, but a performance just the same, a ritual, an offering. Cocktails are an occasion. A little of the past. A little of the future. They're theatre.

And finally they've taken shape before you, teasing eyes around their elegant contours. An olive rolls sideways in crystal clear liquid, 'lazily'; elsewhere colours blush and crushed ice winks; a drop of condensation forms on a frosted glass.

Take the glass, softly, lightly; raise it. A clink, a nod or a knowing glance perhaps; glass touches lips... close your eyes... this is the cocktail moment.

This book is a celebration of the cocktail moment itself, and of what Bombay Sapphire can bring to it.

Gin, a characterful spirit rewarding innovation and respect in equal measure, gives rise to drinks of unmatchable, quintessential style in the hands of Bombay Sapphire. Its unique ingredients, unique manufacturing process, and especially balanced and versatile taste place it in a class of its own when it comes to cocktails.

The book is also a celebration of the past, of tradition and history, the classic cocktails. Of the present: modern twists on those classics. Of place: great bars around the world in which to drink Bombay Sapphire. And of preparation: making it right, the 'just so'.

It features 18 new recipes and advice from Jamie Walker, Head of Mixology at The Bombay Sapphire Experience, Vinopolis, London, plus contributions from the head barmen of featured bars, with their own take on Bombay Sapphire. If we believed that all the best cocktails have already been invented, then the world of cocktail making would be a dull place. But it's not. Who knows, perhaps what you are about to discover are the classics of tomorrow.

IMPORTED
BOMBAY
SAPPHIRE®
Distilled
LONDON
DRY GIN
Distilled from 100%
Grain Neutral Spirit
from a 1761 recipe

GIN IN A COCKTAIL

Gin has a taste. It has character, which means in cocktails there are places you can take it (it loves citrus fruits for example) and there are places you can't. It's not the kind of spirit you can add any old thing to, as you can with some others. It won't stand for that. Instead, and infinitely preferable, it has its own contribution to make. More, it takes centre stage – the alcohol leads the cocktail, and not the other way around. This means that understanding and working with the liquor is crucial, because in so doing it's possible to create a more adult, more complex drink. Yes, it's a challenge. But with challenge comes reward.

The taste of most gins, though not Bombay Sapphire, is heavily influenced by juniper. This is partly due to the choice, number and proportion of the botanicals that flavour the spirit – typically four to six, with, obviously, juniper predominant. It's also partly due to the manufacturing process, which generally sees the botanicals heated in a copper still with the grain spirit and purified water, and then left to steep, to remove their essential oils. Taste is also influenced by the spirit itself, which is commonly grape, molasses, or grain spirit. Grain is the most superior.

BOMBAY SAPPHIRE IN A COCKTAIL

While of course there are other gins of unquestionably good quality, all have a predominance of at least one or two flavours. Bombay Sapphire's recipe and sophisticated distillation process deliver a gin of extraordinary balance and smoothness, where no single ingredient dominates. Which is especially good news where cocktails are concerned.

Gin is the centre of the drink. Different ingredients bring out different qualities in the gin. The idea is to complement them, not mask them. With so many different facets to explore, Bombay Sapphire really is a playground to a skillful drinks maker. It's versatile, because it's less dominated by juniper. It's subtle. It's smooth. With the right combinations, different aspects of its character can be brought forward, in the way a piece of music might allow us to hear a whole orchestra together, but distinctly catch the strain of an oboe or a violin above all the other instruments.

THE CREATION OF BOMBAY SAPPHIRE

Bombay Sapphire differs from other gins in two vital ways: its recipe, and its manufacturing technique. It's these differences that single it out as an ideal cocktail spirit.

Bombay Sapphire uses a unique blend of ten botanicals chosen regardless of cost from all around the world. The quantities are carefully balanced so that no single flavour predominates, according to a 1761 recipe. Skill is involved here, as crops vary from harvest to harvest, and there is quite an art and responsibility to the role of Master Distiller.

The spirit used for Bombay Sapphire is 100% natural grain spirit, of the same quality as that used in the finest malt whiskies, since it is the best carrier of flavours. Despite its exceptional quality, it is triple distilled alone, to remove even the slightest trace of impurities. Only then is it ready for the process proper.

With Bombay Sapphire one key advantage is the distillation itself. Unlike other gins, the spirit is boiled alone in a Carterhead Still. The vapours rise, and are infused through a copper basket containing the botanicals, so flavouring the gin. This process is called Vapour Infusion. It's delicate, for one thing, and it allows control, for another. The Master Distiller can taste and adjust. Only four Carterhead Stills are in existence, and all are used exclusively by the Bombay Spirits company.

This distillation process is slower and more expensive. Other gins take six hours or so to distil, producing 10,000 litres of finished product. Each Bombay Sapphire distillation takes eight hours, producing only half the volume of complete product. All gins are diluted after distillation, Bombay Sapphire by only the purest Welsh spring water. Smoothness, balance, and an eye for detail: Bombay Sapphire strives for perfection at every turn.

Almonds
From Spain

Cubeb Berries
From Java

THE TEN BOTANICALS IN BOMBAY SAPPHIRE

Almonds Spanish almonds are ground to release their precious oils, which are then refined and added to the other botanicals. A clean, strong taste is brought to the mix and more than a hint of nuttiness adds strength to the overall spirit.

Angelica The ground root of the angelica plant is added to help emphasise and complement the flavours of the other botanicals. Its sweet, dry, pine kernel flavour helps to hold the botanicals together, enhancing subtlety.

Cassia Bark The tropics of Indo-China are the source of the delicately-flavoured bark of the cassia tree. Its light cinnamon flavour adds a hint of spice and also serves to sweeten and lighten the botanical mix.

Coriander Fresh from Morocco, coriander seeds are ground down to release their complex blend of citrus and spice: more than a suggestion of lemons and oranges, but softened and rounded by the spice.

Cubeb Berries Fresh from Java, this climbing plant bears pungent, medicinal-smelling berries. When crushed and processed these add a dry, hot, almost mentholated flavour to the spirit. It brings the finishing touch of pepper and pine to the blend.

Grains of Paradise Each of the many flavours in these African grains has a purpose: pepper for bite, lavender for a light, sweet smell, chocolate for that touch of luxury and orange to highlight and accentuate the citrus. In short, they add some of the spice and essence of Africa.

Juniper Berries The best Italian juniper berries add the scent and taste of pine cones, lavender and camphor to the botanical mix. This is the ingredient that gives Bombay Sapphire its dry, fragrant taste.

Lemon Peel We use only the juiciest Spanish lemons, selecting the finest peel to add the most delicate, bittersweet flavour whose freshness and subtlety both lifts the aromas of the rest of the botanicals and helps create Bombay Sapphire's distinctive citrus flavour.

Liquorice Strong, fresh liquorice roots from China add depth to the lighter flavours of the other botanicals. Only the finest root is used in the distillation process, accentuating this cool and highly distinctive aspect.

Orris Orris root adds the scent of violets to Bombay Sapphire and brings in the essence of the warm earth of Italy. It adds an exotic fragrance and helps bind together the other flavours in Bombay Sapphire.

Grains of Paradise
From West Africa

Juniper Berries
From Italy

Lemon Peel
From Spain

Liquorice
From China

Orris
(Iris Root)
From Italy

THE COCKTAIL AGE

Classic cocktails are of lasting interest or significance, of acknowledged excellence: a role model of their kind. They don't become that way by accident. There has to be a certain something. They must be sublime in the taste, have simplicity, elegance and balance. And fashion? A classic is beyond that, untouched by change. But there's more. They carry with them a history, the flavour of an age, the echo of another time, another place. In the case of the martini there is a hint of mystery. And nothing is as alluring as an unanswered question...

Classic cocktails, the martini in particular, are most strongly associated with the 20's and 30's. The First World War had ended. Suppressed frustrations were giving rise to growth, and change. Optimism was in the air, anything seemed possible. Times were moving on. Sexual and social politics were shifting. It was an age of opulence, romance and style. Choose the right glass. Mix a martini, ice cold. Garnish it well, and hold it up to the light. Those qualities are still there.

THE COCKTAIL HOUR

In an atmosphere of change, it's no surprise that the idea of taking tea at five o'clock was a vulnerable one. The new generation had something a little more adventurous in mind. The cocktail hour. More relaxed, more daring. A little time to unwind before the dinner and the dancing, a new way to interact. With it came new concepts of style and fashion. Less formal for the men. Short haircuts for the ladies, dresses that barely touched the knee, layers of chiffon.

The cocktail age meant good taste in more ways than one. The palette was sophisticated: people could distinguish their martinis through garnish alone. Bartenders made their own grenadine and cordials. Drinks were savoured, time was taken. And in America between 1920 and 1933 cocktails had an even greater edge. The element of risk.

Due to prohibition, they were illegal.

THE COCKTAIL MOMENT

Clear as crystal they may be, but all martinis come with a hint of mystery. No one knows the exact moment they were invented. No one can even be quite sure where.

Some credit the celebrated French court composer J.P.A. Martini with a 1763 cocktail of gin and white wine. Much later, others say Jerry Thomas, bartender of San Francisco's Occidental Hotel, made a recipe for a traveller heading to the gold-mining town of Martinez. It called for a dash of bitters, a couple of dashes of Maraschino, a whole glass of vermouth, ice and a pony of Old Tom gin, as laid out in Thomas' own 1887 bartenders' guide. A second theory concerning the town of Martinez has a gold miner in 1870 walking into Julio Richelieu's bar to buy a bottle of whiskey. The nugget of gold he offered as payment was large, so he demanded another drink. Richelieu popped an olive in the drink before handing it over, and dubbed it a 'Martinez'.

Some say the drink was named after the Martini-Henry rifle used by the British army between 1871 and 1891 because the two shared something of a kick. The word martini itself is to be found in the "New and Improved Illustrated Bartenders' Manual or How To Mix Drinks' of the Present Style," by Harry Johnson in 1888. Two others stand closer to the dry martinis we know and love today. In 1896 Tomas Stewart published his "Stewart's Fancy Drinks and How To Mix Them". One cocktail called for two-thirds Plymouth gin, and one-third vermouth, with a dash of orange bitters, though he called it a "Marquerite" rather than a martini. Finally, and possibly most plausibly, comes Martini di Arma di Taggia, head barman of the Knickerbocker Hotel in New York. He mixed equal measures of London Gin and Noilly Prat Vermouth with orange bitters. Then he chilled the drink on ice and strained it into a cold glass. Regulars at the Knickerbocker added the olive.

We'll never know for sure. All we have is what we see and taste and feel: clarity, stillness, perfection. Fire and ice, a moment, just a moment, of salvation. And it's this that lives on.

BOMBAY SAPPHIRE CLASSIC MARTINIS

Bombay Sapphire Classic Martini

Stir 25ml Martini vermouth with ice in a mixing glass and strain to discard excess vermouth, leaving only a coating on the ice. Pour 60ml Bombay Sapphire into the mixing glass containing coated ice, stir and strain into a frosted glass. Garnish with a twist of lemon or a single olive. Alternatively garnish with a double olive to create a Franklin martini. If the mixture is shaken before pouring it becomes a Bradford martini. If it is served without a garnish it becomes a Dickens martini. Add a quarter shot of brine from the cocktail olives to the mixture to create the Dirty martini.

Bombay Sapphire Claridge Classic Martini

Stir 25ml Martini vermouth with ice in a mixing glass and strain to discard excess vermouth, leaving only a coating on the ice. Pour 60ml Bombay Sapphire, 20ml Triple Sec and 20ml Apricot Brandy into the mixing glass containing coated ice, stir and strain into a frosted glass. Garnish with lemon peel. This recipe combines Bombay Sapphire for strength, martini vermouth for dryness and liqueur for sweetness, creating an interesting flavour and taste combination.

Bombay Sapphire Breakfast Martini

Stir 25ml Martini vermouth with ice in a mixing glass and strain to discard excess vermouth, leaving only a coating on the ice. Pour 60ml Bombay Sapphire, 15ml of freshly squeezed lemon juice and one teaspoon of light orange marmalade into the mixing glass containing coated ice, stir and strain into a frosted glass. Garnish with orange peel. This recipe was created by Mr. Salvatore Calabrese at the Lanesborough Hotel Library Bar.

Bombay Sapphire Gibson Martini

Stir 25ml Martini vermouth with ice in a mixing glass and strain to discard excess vermouth, leaving only a coating on the ice. Pour 60ml Bombay Sapphire into the mixing glass containing coated ice, stir and strain into a frosted glass. Garnish with two cocktail onions on a stick.

Bombay Sapphire Gimlet

Stir 25ml Martini vermouth with ice in a mixing glass and strain to discard excess vermouth, leaving only a coating on the ice. Pour 60ml Bombay Sapphire, 25ml lime cordial and 15ml water (optional) into the mixing glass containing coated ice, stir and strain into a frosted glass. Garnish with a lime wedge. This recipe adds the pleasing zip of lime to the Bombay Sapphire Classic martini.

BOMBAY SAPPHIRE CLASSIC COCKTAILS

The Bombay Bramble

Shake 50ml Bombay Sapphire, 25ml freshly-squeezed lemon and 15ml sugar syrup vigorously with ice then strain into a rocks glass filled with crushed ice. Pour the Créme de Mûre slowly into the centre of the glass, allowing it to sink through the mix into the base of the glass. Garnish with a fresh blackberry. This was one of the best and most popular cocktails created in the 1990's.

The Cosmopolitan

Mix 40ml Bombay Sapphire, 25ml Cointreau, 25ml cranberry juice and 15ml lime juice with cracked ice in a shaker and strain into a chilled cocktail glass. Garnish with orange peel. This creates a strong, fruity cocktail with a softened edge.

The French 75

Shake 20ml Bombay Sapphire, 15ml freshly-squeezed lemon juice and 15ml sugar syrup with ice and strain into a glass, then top up with champagne and lightly stir. This cocktail was created by Harry MacElhone in 1925. It was named after the 75 field gun used by the French army during World War One.

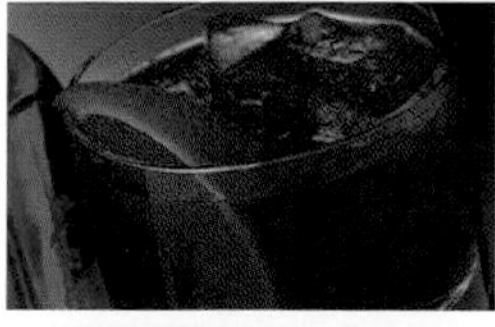

The Negroni

Stir the 25ml Bombay Sapphire, 25ml Martini Bitters, 25ml Martini Rosso vermouth over cracked ice in an old fashioned heavy rocks glass. Top up with soda and garnish with a slice of orange. This drink was named after Count Negroni from Florence, who wanted an Americano 'with a bit more kick'. Bitter and dry, but an extremely refreshing and very tasty drink.

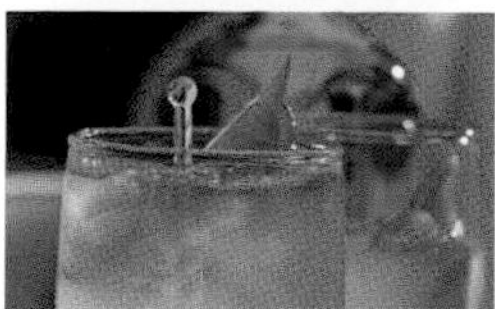

Tom Collins

Shake 60ml of Bombay Sapphire, 30ml of freshly-squeezed lemon juice and 15ml sugar syrup with ice and strain into a 12oz Collins glass. Garnish with a lemon slice. This is classic Bombay Sapphire refreshment.

BOMBAY SAPPHIRE EXPERIENCE AT VINOPOLIS

Vinopolis is London's premiere wine attraction, situated on a two and a half acre site on the vibrant South Bank. It offers an imaginative, interactive tour around the whole world of wine. It's educational, fun, and offers great tastings. The setting is delightful: Victorian vaulted ceilings and intricate, almost rustic red brickwork.

Within is the Bombay Sapphire Experience, and the contrast couldn't be greater. Ice white flooring leads you to an electric blue bar, modern and stylish. The space is given over to exploring at close hand the delights of Bombay Sapphire. Run your hands through containers of the ten botanicals, smell them in their raw form. See a Carterhead Still, see how Bombay Sapphire is made, see the winners of its cocktail glass competitions. And then try a cocktail from Bombay Sapphire mixologist Jamie Walker.

1763 martini

THE 1763 MARTINI

The 1763 martini began with the marriage of gin and wine.

With the huge improvements in both gin and wine production, not to mention the delicacies Bombay Sapphire has to offer, or the fact that so many good wines were close at hand, Jamie Walker was struck by a thought. Was this relationship between gin and wine worth a second, closer look? He decided to experiment with many different wines, to see how they would compliment Bombay Sapphire's subtle nuances. Could they be coaxed down the aisle together, again, nearly two and a half centuries later?

They could. Very happily, as it happens: some wines are a better compliment than others, but at least seven work exceedingly well, creating arrangements that are simultaneously contemporary and retro, the fruits of the wine providing the perfect foil to Bombay Sapphire's citrus edge.

The method for each is the same. Place 25ml of the desired wine in an ice-filled cocktail shaker (use the glass half in order to minimise warming through heat conduction). Pour 50 ml of Bombay Sapphire over the ice and wine. Stir until the mixture is ice cold. This should take about 20 seconds. Strain your cocktail into a pre-chilled martini glass.

The results are startling. 7 matches made in heaven. Ladies and gentlemen… all rise for the Bombay Sapphire 1763 martinis.

IMPORTED
BOMBAY
SAPPHIRE
Distilled
LONDON
DRY GIN
Distilled from 100%
Grain Neutral Spirit
from a 1761 recipe
PRODUCT OF ENGLAND
IMPORTED

Bombay Sapphire '1763' Martini. Dry Riesling
This martini has a light and floral aroma with honeyed hints floating above it. The wine is crisply dry on the palate with sweetish floral notes like honeysuckle and rose petal. Combining this with Bombay Sapphire creates a limy zing of acidity with a refreshing finish, including notes of tropical fruits on the front of the palate. This martini is complimented wonderfully with a twist of grapefruit or lime.

Bombay Sapphire '1763' Martini. Faber Pinot Noir
This recipe delivers a light, sweet martini with hints of dry earthy minerals behind a 'grapey' palate.
A citrus twist adds another layer of depth.

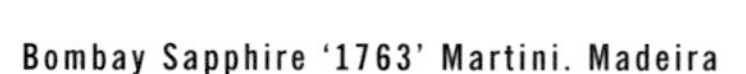

Bombay Sapphire '1763' Martini. Madeira
Toffee and caramel aromas from this wine lend themselves beautifully to Bombay Sapphire's layers of citrus and light spice. The result is a rich digestive-style cocktail with a nutty, caramel and slightly stewed flavour that brings out a wonderfully sweet, rich, fruitcake flavour on the palate.

Bombay Sapphire '1763' Martini. Zinfandel
A soft lush martini is created with Zinfandel - the wine itself is rich and ripe with summer fruits and spicy, white pepper hints and rich, creamy vanilla notes.

Bombay Sapphire '1763' Martini. Pedro Ximinez Sherry
An intensely sweet wine which is thick and syrupy, with rich and unctuous flavours of honey, toffee, caramel and bananas, which in the martini itself provide the perfect counterfoil to Bombay Sapphire's crisp citrus edge.

Bombay Sapphire '1763' Martini. Amarone
A martini of some richness, with a nose of sour cherries and chocolate notes and plums and bitter cherries that linger on the palate. Always use a good quality Amarone.

Bombay Sapphire '1763' Martini. Sauvignon Blanc
A highly aromatic wine with rich elements of pea pod and asparagus, with dry and tart green fruits dominating. The Bombay Sapphire draws on these characteristics to create a cocktail with grassy, gooseberry and nettle notes. Its citrus elements carry it to a refreshing finish.

BOMBAY S

JAMIE WALKER

Jamie Walker has been shaking and stirring up cocktails, and people's perception of them for the duration of his adult life.

He has run several of London's top cocktail bars, including Circus, Opium, and Alphabet. As a consultant, he has trained staff at several more, including the Lab Bar, Ten Room, Sanderson, Atlantic, Detroit, West St, Amber and 23 Romily Street.

He's hosted bar seminars throughout Europe, and in the United States.

His philosophy is simple. By respecting and understanding your ingredients you can learn how to combine them to achieve the most important thing in a cocktail: balance of flavours. It's a matter of questioning, and a question of practice. With understanding comes confidence. Barmen like to make their job seem harder than it is. Snobbery dictates that drinks can only be a certain way. Not so. The ingredients have to be respected. Beyond that, you do it your way. Experiment, be adventurous, get things wrong, challenge the rules, make the recipes your own. The cocktail moment should belong to you. You own it. And let no barman tell you otherwise.

JAMIE WALKER'S SAPPHIRE FACETS

The following three drinks are aromatic without being overtly perfumed. Bold, yet subtle, and perfectly balanced.

Bombay Finbar

Sapphire and Emerald

Bombay Scratch

BOMBAY FINBAR

Shake 50ml of Bombay Sapphire, 25ml of ginger and lemongrass cordial and 50ml of mango juice vigorously with ice and strain into an ice-filled glass.

Fill to the top with lemonade and garnish the cocktail with a lemon slice and a straw made from a hollowed length of lemongrass.

SAPPHIRE AND EMERALD

Carefully select a suitable highball glass and fill with ice. We recommend using a blue-tinted glass for this recipe if one is available.

Place 25ml of Bombay Sapphire, 25ml Creme de Menthe Verte and 25ml of Absinthe into the iced highball. Top up the mixture with lemonade, stirring gently.

This cocktail looks its best when garnished with a lime wedge.

SAPPHIRE SCRATCH

Select 3 leaves of basil, 3 leaves of mint and 3 leaves of coriander and place into the base of a cocktail shaker. Add a dash of sugar syrup and a squeeze of lemon then, muddle the mixture.

Add 75ml of Bombay Sapphire and fill the shaker with cubed ice. Stir until the mixture is sufficiently chilled then 'double strain' into a shallow martini glass using a tea strainer to remove any residual herbs. Garnish with torn basil leaves.

Miami
1220
TIDES

South Beach, Miami. Beautiful people, beautiful bars, beautiful drinks – it's gone off on its own one-location definition of the ultimate in cocktails.

At the mellow end of the scale, silky live jazz weaves its magic at The Tides, where vibrant, snappily dressed cocktail lovers sip remarkable martinis in a contemporary, but highly romantic setting, overlooking the ocean.

Karim Rashid
Dry martini with olive garnish.

Tides
Miami

Michael Graves
Dry martini with a twist of lemon.

The lounge bar

Design celebrity Karim Rashid rose to worldwide pre-eminence with his organic futurism aesthetic, and his diverse clientele ranges from Issey Miyake to Yahoo! "An organic glass floats supported only at one tenuous point by a silver pinnacle the olive is pierced on. It is presented like a beacon of the best drink available to mankind, the Bombay Sapphire martini."

Known for his cultural and educational projects, Michael Graves' institutional work covers the globe. Graves has designed products for many of the world's leading manufacturers, including Alessi, Duravit and Target. His martini glass for Bombay Sapphire exemplifies his award-winning style: tradition with a twist.

Marcel Wanders
Dry martini with olive garnish.

Tides
Miami

Vladimir Kagan
Dry martini.

Wanders' knack for transforming ordinary objects and materials into extraordinary items has pushed this Dutch designer to the top of his field. Known for pieces like his Knotted Chair and Egg Vase, Wanders' contribution to the Bombay Sapphire martini glass perfectly illustrates his humourous yet refined design aesthetic.

The pool

Vladimir Kagan's history includes commissions for the delegates' cocktail lounges at the first UN headquarters, to seating for all of Tom Ford's Gucci stores.
"The glass is an artistic homage to my favourite drink, The Bombay Sapphire martini, dry and cold... bruised not stirred... straight-up... enjoyed sip by sip! "

JAMIE WALKER'S SAPPHIRE DECADENCE

This section is compiled of drinks boasting eccentric ingredients that when balanced correctly create a wonderfully opulent tipple.

Black Antoinette

Black Forest Sapphire

Bombay Drago

BLACK ANTOINETTE

Build 25ml of Bombay Sapphire, 25ml Sambuca and 25ml of blackberry puree into the glass then top up with champagne, stirring gently as you do so. It is essential to chill the ingredients before adding the champagne.

Solid pressed stem with blown bowl 'touch' barware designed by Jessamy Kelly.

BLACK FOREST SAPPHIRE

Place 50ml of Bombay Sapphire, 25ml of Mozart dark chocolate liqueur, 15ml of cherry syrup, 4 black cherries and 75ml of thick vanilla yoghurt into a blender with a scoop of crushed ice. Blend until smooth then pour gently into a large glass. Top up with thick cream or yoghurt and garnish with a cherry.

BOMBAY DRAGO

Shake 50ml Bombay Sapphire, 25ml of beef consome and 15ml of pickled beetroot juice vigorously with ice and strain into a chilled martini glass. Pour sour cream over the back of a bar spoon to create a swirl on the surface of the drink.

London

Art Bar

Townhouse

London's South Kensington and Knightsbridge are home to Art Bar and the Townhouse, along with a host of well-known and fashionable stores. This stylish area provides the opportunity to explore the ultimate in London chic.

The cocktails created for Bombay Sapphire By Jens Encle and Kaziu Hajee of Art Bar and Will de la Praudiere at Townhouse draw upon some of the finest and freshest ingredients to create recipes that are sublime in taste and classic in their presentation.

These can be enjoyed in the gallery surroundings at Art Bar with exhibits adorning the walls for enjoyment and for purchase, or with some equally ingenious recipes from the kitchen in the personal and private surroundings at Townhouse.

Sapphire Together

6 fresh raspberries muddled
50ml Bombay Sapphire
25ml Chambourd
Dash Framboise
Dash sugar syrup
Top up with champagne

Art Bar

South Kensington, London

Sapphire Shini

50ml Bombay Sapphire
Dash of apple schnapps
Large dash of lychee liqueur
Large dash of apple juice
Dash of sours

Muddle the raspberries in the base of a shaker with Bombay Sapphire, Chambourd, Framboise and sugar syrup. Shake with ice and then pour into a pair of tall shot glasses. Top up with champagne and garnish each glass with two raspberries on a cocktail stick.

Mr. Jens Encle
Mixologist

Mr. Kaziu Hajee
Mixologist

Pour all the ingredients into an ice-filled cocktail shaker then stir them together. Pour into a chilled martini glass and garnish with a lychee or fresh raspberry gently dropped into the cocktail.

Monarch

Bombay Sapphire
Lemon juice
Elderflower cordial
Dash of peach bitters
Teaspoon of sugar

Townhouse
Knightsbridge, London

Elderflower Collins

Bombay Sapphire
Elderflower cordial
Lemon juice
Sugar syrup
Maraschino

Pour all the ingredients into an ice-filled shaker and shake vigorously. Strain into a chilled martini glass and garnish with lemon shavings.

Mr. Will de la Praudiere
Mixologist

Pour the ingredients into an ice-filled shaker and mix together. Fill an elegant highball glass with crushed ice and pour the ingredients into the glass. Top up with soda water and garnish with lemon shavings and a sprig of mint. Serve with a straw.

JAMIE WALKER'S SAPPHIRE COMFORTERS

These three recipes create warming comfort drinks not necessarily seasonal, but positively festive.

The Elegant Ellis

Keats Sapphire

Wenceslas Sapphire

THE ELEGANT ELLIS

Muddle 1 diced skin of a clementine in syrup with the vanilla sugar at the bottom of a rocks glass or highball glass. Fill the glass with crushed ice. Shake 50ml of ginger-infused Bombay Sapphire, the juice of half a mandarin and a dash of lime juice vigorously in a Boston shaker and strain into the glass. Stir gently and garnish with a clementine segment.

THE KEATS SAPPHIRE

Shake 25ml of Bombay Sapphire, 25ml of Cointreau, 15ml of spiced berry cordial and 15ml of cranberry juice vigorously with ice and strain into a rocks glass filled with crushed ice. Garnish with seasonal berries.

WENCESLAS SAPPHIRE

Muddle one pitted date and one fig with 75ml of Bombay Sapphire in the bottom of your cocktail shaker. Add 25ml of fresh pressed apple juice and 15ml of single cream. Shake vigorously with ice and strain into a chilled martini glass.

Tokyo
B-bar
The Peak bar

There is an increasing demand in Japan, and Tokyo in particular, for bars which have impeccable interior design, perfect atmosphere and a desirable location to meet the needs of ever more sophisticated customers. Surroundings are everything. The B-bar and The Peak Bar are two well-established and popular venues that answer these needs exactly.

Bombay Sapphire is popular mixed with Perrier, on the rocks and as the key to the perfect martini. Bartenders and mixologists in Tokyo are creating many new cocktails, in particular new martinis with liqueurs or fresh fruit. The Tokyo cocktails featured have been especially created for Bombay Sapphire by Mr. Satoshi Yamauchi of the B-bar and Ms. Ayami Yokokawa of The Peak Bar.

The B-bar
Roppongi Hills Tokyo

Shérazade

Bombay Sapphire
Dry vermouth
Maraschino
Cranberry jelly
Lemon peel

Hortensia

Bombay Sapphire
Kyoho (Japanese Muscat) juice
Tonic water

Place cranberry jelly into the martini glass. Stir Bombay Sapphire with dry vermouth and maraschino then pour into glass. Garnish with lemon peel if desired.

Served in a Baccarat Harcourt Small Wine.

Pour Bombay Sapphire and Kyoho juice into an ice-filled shaker. Shake ingredients and pour into a champagne flute. Top up with tonic water then add Kyoho juice gently allowing it to settle on the bottom of the glass.

Served in a Baccarat Massena Champagne Flute.

Mr. Satoshi Yamauchi
Mixologist

The Peak Bar
Park Hyatt Tokyo

Frozen Martini

45ml Bombay Sapphire
30ml Grapefruit liqueur
30ml Fresh grapefruit juice
2 teaspoons of brown sugar

Combine the ingredients in a blender with 2 cups of crushed ice. Pour into a chilled martini glass and garnish with fresh grapefruit and mint leaves.

Citruschka

60ml Bombay Sapphire
60ml Cranberry juice
Peeled and quartered orange wedges
2 teaspoons of brown sugar

Muddle orange wedges in the bottom of a shaker with the brown sugar. Fill the shaker with crushed ice and add Bombay Sapphire and cranberry juice. Shake and strain into a highball glass. Serve with a straw if desired.

Ms. Ayami Yokokawa
Mixologist

JAMIE WALKER'S NATURAL SAPPHIRES

These three recipes harness the power of nature: sometimes forceful, sometimes delicate, sometimes eccentric.

Sapphire Shogun

Rosemary's Sapphire Infusion

Barbed Bombay

THE SAPPHIRE SHOGUN

Shake 50ml of Bombay Sapphire, 25ml of sake, 25ml of V8 juice and a dash of Wasabi vigorously with ice and strain into a chilled martini glass. Garnish with a lime wedge.

ROSEMARY'S SAPPHIRE INFUSION

Shake 50ml of rosemary infused Bombay Sapphire, 25ml of Jaffa orange juice and 15ml of Grand Marnier vigorously with ice and strain into a chilled martini glass. Garnish with a Jaffa orange flame.

BARBED BOMBAY

Muddle rhubarb and gomme at the bottom of a large highball glass. Place a scoop of ice in the glass. Add 50ml of Bombay Sapphire, 25ml of rhubarb sake, 1 heaped barspoon of stewed rhubarb and a dash of sugar syrup. Top up the glass with ginger.

London

Cicada

Vic Naylor

Clerkenwell, London, is one of the city's most fashionable areas. It has a vibrant and varied community with many bars, art galleries and other nightlife centred on and around Charterhouse and St John Street. Vic Naylor and Cicada are well-established bars whose staff are constantly seeking out the very best in cocktails and experiment regularly with fresh ingredients to bring their customers new discoveries. Both bars are attached to restaurants providing food of the highest quality to compliment the mixologists' expertise. The cocktails featured have been chosen by the mixologists Ben Alderman at Cicada and Spencer Collins at Vic Naylor exclusively for Bombay Sapphire.

Cicada
St John Street, London

Nashi Pear Martini
25ml Bombay Sapphire
25ml Sake (silver)
25ml Poire Williams Liqueur
50ml pear puree
A dash of lemon juice
A dash of sugar syrup

French Martini
40ml Bombay Sapphire
20ml lemon juice
10ml sugar syrup
Float Crème de Mure

Place all the ingredients into an ice-filled shaker and shake vigorously together. Pour into a chilled martini glass and garnish with a slice of pear on a cocktail stick on the rim of the glass.

Mr. Ben Alderman
Mixologist

Pour the Bombay Sapphire, Lemon juice and sugar syrup into an ice-filled shaker. Shake together vigorously then pour into a chilled martini glass. Float the Crème de Mure onto the surface of the cocktail and garnish with a twist of lemon.

Vic Naylor
St John Street, London

Hungarian Passion
40ml Bombay Sapphire
Half glass Champagne
25ml Passionfruit puree
15ml Creme de Mure
15ml Passionfruit syrup
15ml Lime, 15ml sugar syrup

Mint Sapphire Collins
15-20 leaves of fresh mint
50ml Bombay Sapphire
50ml Lemon juice
25ml sugar syrup

Take a large rocks or highball glass and fill with crushed ice. Half-fill with champagne. Shake the remaining ingredients with ice in a shaker then pour over the crushed ice. Gently stir the cocktail then garnish with half a fresh passionfruit and a sprig of mint.

Mr. Spencer Waterman
Mixologist

Muddle the mint and gomme together in the base of the glass long enough to just break the leaves. Add Bombay Sapphire, lemon juice and ice. Top up with soda then gently stir to mix the cocktail. Garnish with a large sprig of mint.

JAMIE WALKER'S SAPPHIRE SPECIALTIES

These are playful cocktails that still contain a measure of sophistication and complexity.

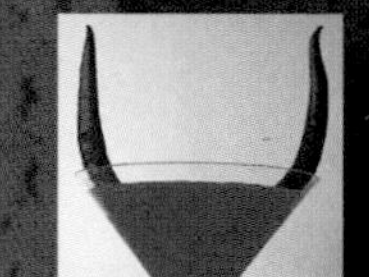

Masked Devil of Bombay

Bombay Rouge

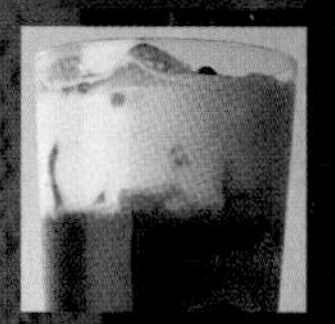

Starsky Sapphire

MASKED DEVIL OF BOMBAY

Muddle the lemongrass stalk, melon segments and chilli in a Boston shaker. Add 25ml of Bombay Sapphire, 25ml of melon liqueur and ice.

Shake the ingredients together vigorously and pour into a chilled martini glass.

Garnish with two 'split' chilli horns on the rim.

BOMBAY ROUGE

Pour 35ml of Bombay Sapphire, 15ml framboise liqueur, 50ml cranberry / blackberry juice, a dash of lime, a dash of gomme, and a dash of orange bitters into your preferred shaker. Shake all the ingredients vigorously with ice. Strain into a highball glass filled with ice. Garnish with a fresh raspberry to create a richly refreshing cocktail.

THE STARSKY SAPPHIRE

Build 25ml of Bombay Sapphire, 25ml of coffee liqueur and 50ml of single cream over ice straight into your preferred highball glass. Stir with a bar spoon and top up with root beer.

Barcelona & Madrid

The curiosity and inventiveness of cocktail lovers has resulted in the existence of a variety of great drinks. Spain has a long cocktail tradition, and considers itself a leader in the field. The world of cocktails here has evolved thanks to great barmen: from the great Boadas, with his daughter Mª Dolores following firmly in his footsteps, to the charismatic Pedro Chicote and Pedro Carbonell; José Victori; Pablo Casas; Jose Mª Gotarde; José Mª Gotarde Jr.; Manuel Trivió. The list is endless. The wisdom of these innovators has nourished a new generation of young mixologists, whose work can be sampled in bars, hotels and restaurants the length and breadth of Spain.

Night Cosmopolitan

Dash of natural lime juice
30ml triple sec
60ml Bombay Sapphire
Crème de Mure

Dry Martini
Barcelona

Information

DRY MARTINI
C/ Aribau, 162-166
08036 Barcelona
www.drymartinibcn.com

Eighteen years after creating Dry Martini in 1979, Pedro Carbonell handed over to Javier de las Muelas. Javier brought with him a new concept of modernity, including ambient and chillout music.

Still, Javier de las Muelas has managed to conserve all the original charm by preserving the classical decorations, with considerable importance being given to the atmosphere (gold, wood, leather sofas and the unique barmen's waistcoats).

Consequently, the Dry Martini has opened itself up to a truly varied and heterogeneous clientele of all ages and tastes.

Mix the ingredients with cracked ice in a shaker. Shake together then strain into a chilled martini glass. Garnish with a twist of lime.

Mr. Eduardo Lupiañez
Mixologist

Information

MUSEO CHICOTE
Gran Vía, 12
28013 Madrid

It's rare that a bar gains the kind of immortality which moves it to outlive and survive its founder. Museo Chicote is without a doubt one of these places with the Midas Touch. Since 1931 it's been a landmark on Madrid´s Gran Via and its history is dotted with all kinds of stories. It's founder, Pedro Chicote, managed to combine the skill of concocting the most exquisite mixtures of alcohol with a natural gift for public relations and a tolerance and cosmopolitan attitude unusual for this period. The result is this Art Déco jewel of the Gran Via.

Museo Chicote is again a place enjoyed by all kinds of people of all ages, with one common denominator: the love of cocktails.

Museo Chicote
Madrid

Mr. Agustín Vivas
Mixologist

Sapphire Compuesta

3 parts Bombay Sapphire
2 parts Martini Rosso
1 shot of Benedictine
Red Curaçao
Grand Marnier
Pineapple syrup

Place a few leaves of mint, a red morello cherry and a green morello cherry in a tumbler. Crush ice and add a dash of Red Curaçao, Grand Marnier and Pineapple Syrup. Add 3 parts Bombay Sapphire and 2 parts Martini Rosso. Add a slight drop of Benedictine liquer and finish off with a slice of lemon and orange.

JAMIE WALKER'S SAPPHIRE LUXURIES

The following drinks are decadent and fun. But follow the recipes closely; they're delicately balanced.

Bombay Lemon Bomb

Bombay Split

Sapphire Wozzy

BOMBAY LEMON BOMB

Pour 50ml of Bombay Sapphire, 25ml of limoncello and 1 heaped barspoon of lemon curd into a shaker with one scoop of ice. Shake very vigorously, then pour into a chilled martini glass.

THE BOMBAY SPLIT

Pour 25ml of Bombay Sapphire, 25ml of banana liqueur, 25ml of Galliano, 100ml orange juice, 100ml banana nectar and a dash of grenadine into an ice-filled shaker. Vigorously shake and strain into an ice-filled highball glass.

THE SAPPHIRE WOZZY

Place 50ml of Bombay Sapphire, 50ml Guava Juice, 25ml mango juice, 15ml coconut cream and a dash of lemon juice into a blender with a scoop of ice. Blend until smooth then pour into a rocks or hurricane glass.

Mixology

Bar Tools

Techniques

Mixology is the craft of mixing spirits with other ingredients to create perfect cocktails. And craft it is, which means it takes time and practice. My advice: give yourself a chance. The end result will only be as good as the individual ingredients, so only use the very best: the crispest ice, the freshest, highest-quality mixers, and the most premium of spirits. The same goes for your tools. Whether you're stirring, shaking, blending or muddling – or serving for that matter – make sure you're at ease with your kit, and confident it will never let you down: again, you shouldn't settle for second best. And thirdly, trust your taste; for gaining the confidence to judge for yourself, rather than relying constantly on other people's measures, is one of the most rewarding aspects of mixology.

JAMIE WALKER'S RECOMMENDED BAR TOOLS

Cocktail Shaker

The two-piece Boston Shaker is recommended over the three-piece shaker. This is divided into a metal half (or tin) and a glass half. This type of shaker is superior to the three-piece tin shaker as you can use the glass half to prepare ingredients without conducting warmth in the same way that tin shakers do, thus ensuring an optimally chilled cocktail.

Strainer

The Boston Shaker requires a separate strainer to drain the ingredients into a glass. If necessary, ingredients can be double-strained by holding a tea strainer beneath the regular cocktail strainer. This will remove any smaller, unwanted piths, seeds etc.

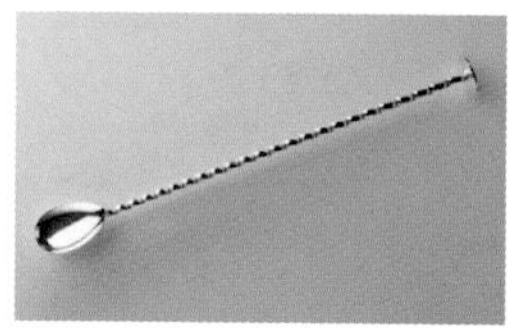

Bar Spoon

A bar spoon is essential for layering and stirring your cocktails. The best ones will have a twisted stem and flat end to enable complete control.

Muddler

A wooden muddler is an important bar tool. If one is not available then the end of a small wooden rolling pin or wooden spoon handle will suffice although this may scar the glass if used too vigorously.

JAMIE WALKER'S TECHNIQUES

Blending Use this technique to create smooth frozen drinks. On the whole, blended drinks will contain more robust ingredients, such as juices, coconut cream and cream. You should place all the cocktail ingredients in the blender and blitz until the mixture is of a smooth consistency. The mixture should be able to hold two straws upright, but not so thick that you need an industrial pump to drink it!

Building the drink This is the simplest method of cocktail creating. Just pour all the ingredients into an ice-filled glass and then give them a quick stir to gently mix them together.

Citrus Flame Take a slightly larger section of skin than required for the twist. The top of the fruit is the best area as it is slightly harder. Hold the skin over the surface of the drink, facing it away from yourself. Take a lighter and warm the outside of the skin for about three seconds, then, keeping the flame lit, squeeze the skin. This will release the oils, which ignite over the drink. This not only looks spectacular but also caramelises the sugars in the fruit, enhancing the cocktail's flavour.

Chilling a martini glass Take a polished martini glass and place a scoop of ice inside. Add water to the brim. Leave to chill whilst mixing your cocktail. When your cocktail is ready to strain, discard the ice from the glass and shake to remove any excess water. By chilling the glass you will extend the life expectancy of the cocktail.

Coring and baking fruit Take your required fruit and starting from the centre at the top of the fruit cut out its core using a downward motion. Discard the core. (Use a corer, if you have one. It is a much easier option, as removing the core from fruit can be tricky using a knife). To bake the desired fruit, slice around its circumference. This prevents the fruit from splitting during baking. Rub the top with a small amount of butter. Place in a baking tray and cook for 20-25 minutes in a pre-heated oven at 200°. Once cooked, leave the fruit to cool and then place in a fridge until required. A squeeze of lime juice over the cooked fruit will aid its longevity. The fruit is now ready to be placed in the glass of the cocktail which accompanies it.

Fruit and Juices As with all ingredients, you should make sure that they are as fresh as possible and of the highest quality. Juices should never be concentrated, but always freshly pressed or squeezed.

JAMIE WALKER'S TECHNIQUES

Fruit coils Take a sharp knife and slice the skin off the fruit starting at the top. In one careful downward movement remove all of its skin. Again be sure to remove as much of the pith as possible. You should now be left with a coil-shaped citrus skin which can be topped or tailed to fit the required glass. Crushed ice should then be placed inside the coil so that it lies neatly against the inside of the glass.

Twists Using a sharp knife remove a section of skin from the required fruit of about 10mm in width and 25mm long. Always remove as much of the pith as possible. Then take a sliver of the skin and 'twist' it over the pre-prepared drink releasing the fruit's essential oils over the surface. Drop the twist into the drink. This gives the cocktail another dimension in flavour as well as being aesthetically pleasing.

Ice Never overlook the importance of ice. It is not only there to chill your drink but is also an integral ingredient. Always use fresh ice (the colder the better) as fresh ice has a more transparent appearance than 'tired weeping ice' which has a hazier look about it. If it is possible, keep ice in a professional ice bucket/well as this ensures that the ice is in a space which allows it to drain. This enables the ice to remain fresh for as long as possible.

Infusing Bombay Sapphire Using cooking gauze, wrap your desired fresh herbs into a cigar shape. Tie both ends of the gauze with string. Feed this garne style parcel into the Bombay Sapphire through the neck of the bottle. Infuse for the required amount of time. (See individual recipes for specific instructions).

Muddling This method uses a muddler to crush and macerate whole fruits, skins, sugars or herbs to release their juices and flavours. This normally takes place in the cocktail glass itself but can also happen in the shaker. If you do not own a muddler, you can use a flat-ended rolling pin.

JAMIE WALKER'S TECHNIQUES

Shake and strain This method works beautifully with libations that contain cream, milk, juices, purees or egg. You should use the maximum amount of ice (again this is to prevent dilution, and shake vigorously) until the metal section of the shaker is well frosted. Vigorous shaking is especially important for cocktails containing egg white, so that the frothy head desired is created. Always use fresh ice in the finished glass as opposed to the ice you have just shaken with and strain the ingredients into the glass using a cocktail strainer.

Spiced sugar Take 500g of plain white sugar. Add 15g of ground nutmeg, 15g ground cinnamon and the seeds from 3 vanilla pods. Stir well. The quantities of spices used can be varied to suit personal tastes.

Stir and strain This method works best for cocktails that need to be treated with a slightly defter hand than a 'shaken' cocktail. Drinks that are stirred should be done with the maximum amount of ice in the glass section of your shaker. This is to stop the drink becoming diluted or 'Bruised'. The stirred ingredients should then be strained using a cocktail strainer into the relevant glass.
('Bruised' – by shaking the drink, shards of ice and pockets of air damage the alcohol).

Sugar nests This is a beautiful and delicious garnish. Place half a cup of sugar in a small saucepan over a low heat. The sugar, after a short time, will turn to liquid (caramel). When this happens, carefully pour the caramel from a good height onto a wooden spoon, twisting the spoon as you go. The liquid sugar will solidify around the spoon as it makes contact with the cold air. The result will be a delightful sugar nest effect. Half a cup of sugar should provide you with enough liquid to make four or five nests.

Stewing rhubarb Place 2 or 3 stalks of rhubarb in a pan with half a cup of water. Add 2 dessert spoons of sugar. Bring to the boil and simmer until soft. This process should take approximately 12 – 15 minutes. Place in a fridge to chill.

THE COCKTAIL INDEX

Page 14
Bombay Sapphire Classic martini

Page 14
Bombay Sapphire Claridge martini

Page 14
Bombay Sapphire Breakfast martini

Page 14
Bombay Sapphire Gibson martini

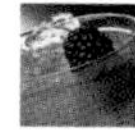
Page 15
The Bombay Bramble

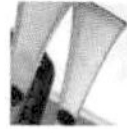
Page 15
The French Seventy Five

Page 15
The Cosmopolitan

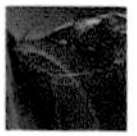
Page 15
The Negroni

Page 15
Tom Collins

Page 20
Bombay Sapphire '1763' martini

Page 21
Dry Riesling

Page 21
Faber Pinot Noir

Page 21
Madeira

Page 21
Zinfandel

Page 21
Pedro Ximinez Sherry

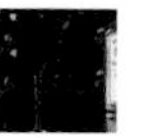
Page 21
Amarone

Page 21
Sauvignon Blanc

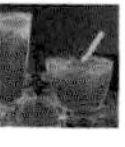
Page 25
Bombay Finbar

Page 26
Sapphire and Emerald

Page 27
Sapphire Scratch

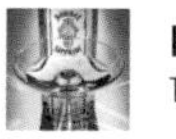
Page 30
Traditional martini's

Page 30
Traditional martini's

Page 31
Traditional martini's

Page 31
Traditional martini's

Page 33
Black Antoinette

Page 34
Black Forest Sapphire

Page 35
Bombay Drago

Page 38
Sapphire Together

Page 38
Sapphire Shini

Page 39
Monarch

THE COCKTAIL INDEX

Page 39
Elderflower Collins

Page 41
Elegant Ellis

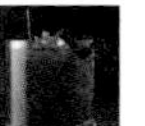
Page 42
The Keats Sapphire

Page 43
Wenceslas Sapphire

Page 46
Shérazade

Page 46
Hortensia

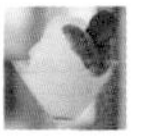
Page 47
Frozen martini

Page 47
Citruska

Page 49
The Sapphire Shogun

Page 50
Rosemary's Sapphire Infusion

Page 51
Barbed Bombay

Page 54
Nashi Pear martini

Page 54
French martini

Page 55
Hungarian Passion

Page 55
Mint Sapphire Collins

Page 57
Masked Devil of Bombay

Page 58
Bombay Rouge

Page 59
The Starsky Sapphire

Page 62
Night Cosmopolitan

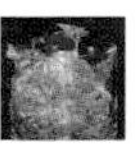
Page 63
Sapphire Compuesta

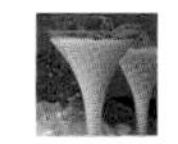
Page 65
Bombay Lemon Bomb

Page 66
Bombay Split

Page 67
Sapphire Wozzy

ACKNOWLEDGEMENTS

CREATIVE CONTRIBUTION

CONSULTANT	Dick Bradsell, London. England.
MIXOLOGY	Jamie Walker, Bombay Sapphire Experience at Vinopolis, London. England.
	Jens Encle, Art Bar, London. England.
	Kaziu Hajee, Art bar, London. England.
	Will de la Praudiere, Townhouse, London. England.
	Ben Alderman, Cicada, London. England.
	Spencer Waterman, Vic Naylor. London. England.
	Satoshi Yamauchi, The B-bar. Roppongi Hills, Tokyo. Japan.
	Ayami Yokokawa, The Peak Bar, Park Hyatt, Tokyo. Japan.
	Eduardo Lupiañez, Dry Martini, Barcelona. Spain.
	Agustín Vivas, Museo Chicote, Madrid. Spain.
DESIGN	Meadow, London. England.
ART DIRECTION	Meadow, London. England.
PHOTOGRAPHY	Martin Langfield, London. England.
	The Bombay Sapphire Image Library.
STYLIST	Emelie Hall, London. England.
COPYWRITER	Scott Perry, London. England.
PRINTING	The Midas Press, Farnborough. England.